To
_____

From
_____

KPT PUBLISHING

THERAPY IN A BOX

Copyright © 2017 KPT Publishing

Published by KPT Publishing
Minneapolis, Minnesota 55406
www.KPTPublishing.com

ISBN 978-1-944833-06-0

Design and Development by
Koechel Peterson and Associates
Minneapolis, Minnesota

Images are courtesy of Shutterstock

First printing March 2017

10 9 8 7 6 5 4 3 2 1

Printed in the United States of America

COLOR YOUR DRIVE HOME

I PUT MY HEART AND MY
SOUL INTO MY WORK,
AND HAVE LOST MY MIND
IN THE PROCESS.

VINCENT VAN GOGH

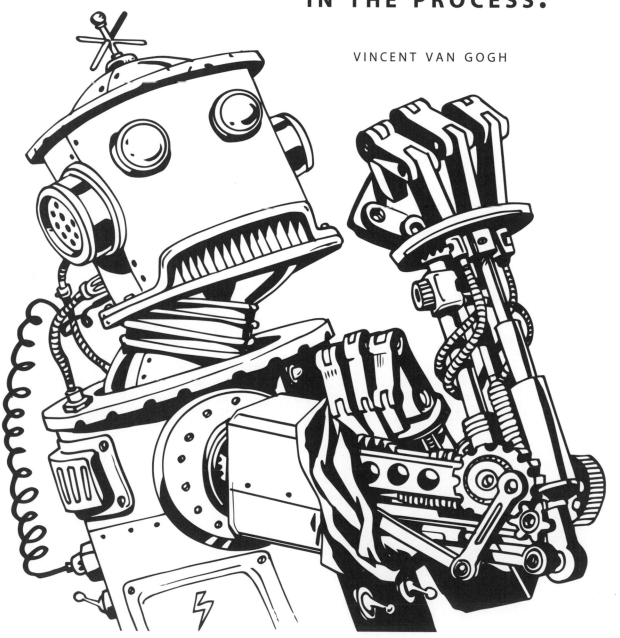

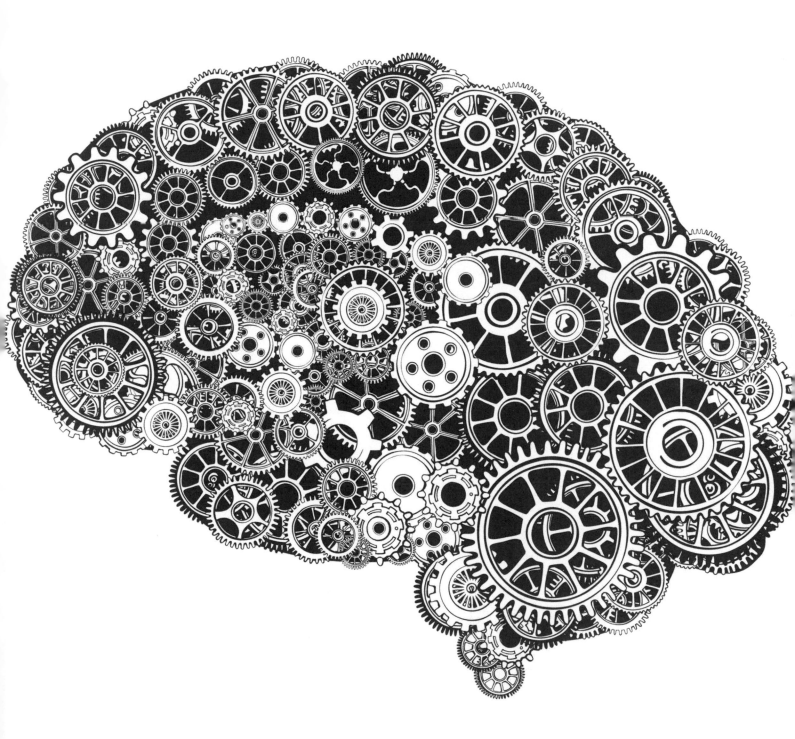

A REMEDY FOR ALMOST ANYTHING IS FAMILY

(GETTING THE DOSAGE CORRECT CAN BE TRICKY)

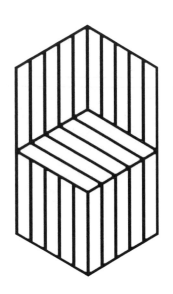

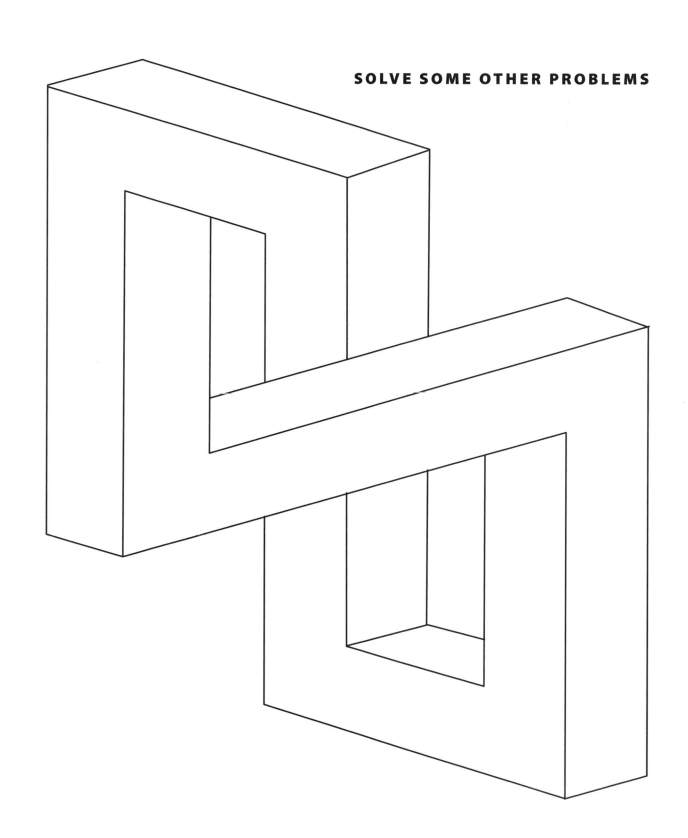

SOLVE SOME OTHER PROBLEMS

PLAN YOUR ESCAPE ROUTE

GET SOME
FRESH AIR

PICK UP A NEW HOBBY

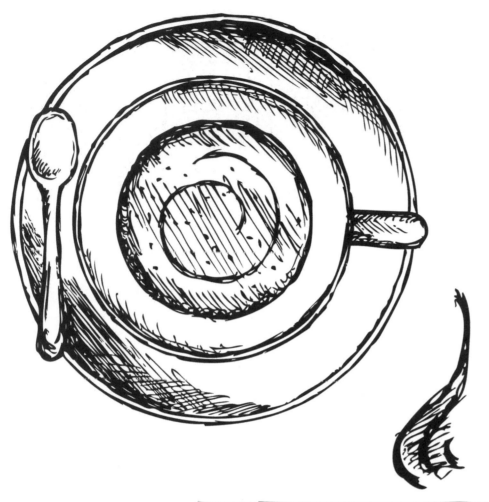

TAKE REGULAR,

SHORT VACATIONS

(AS IN 15 MINUTES).

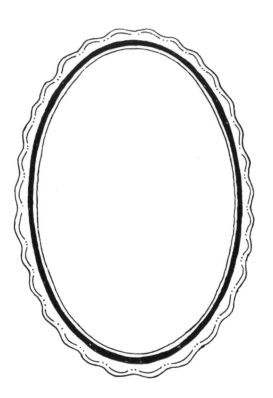

HANDMADE
Soap
100% natural

SOAP
Lavender
HANDMADE WITH LOVE

SOAP
Collection

HANDMADE
SOAP
ALL NATURAL

ALL NATURAL
SEA SALT
HANDMADE SOAP

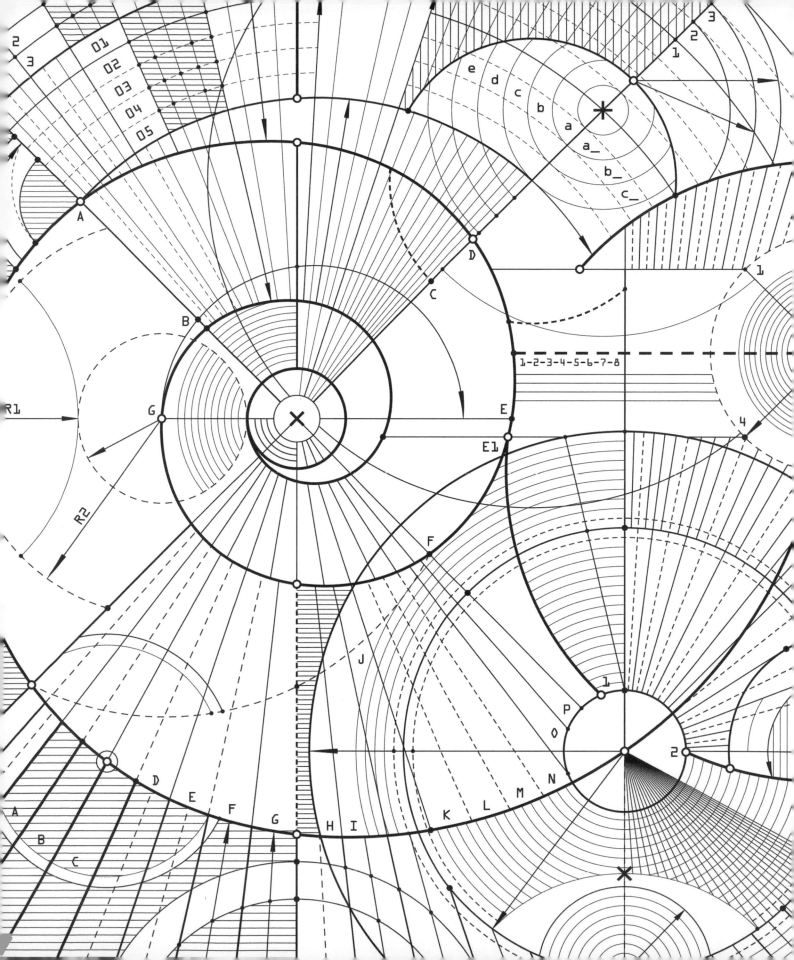

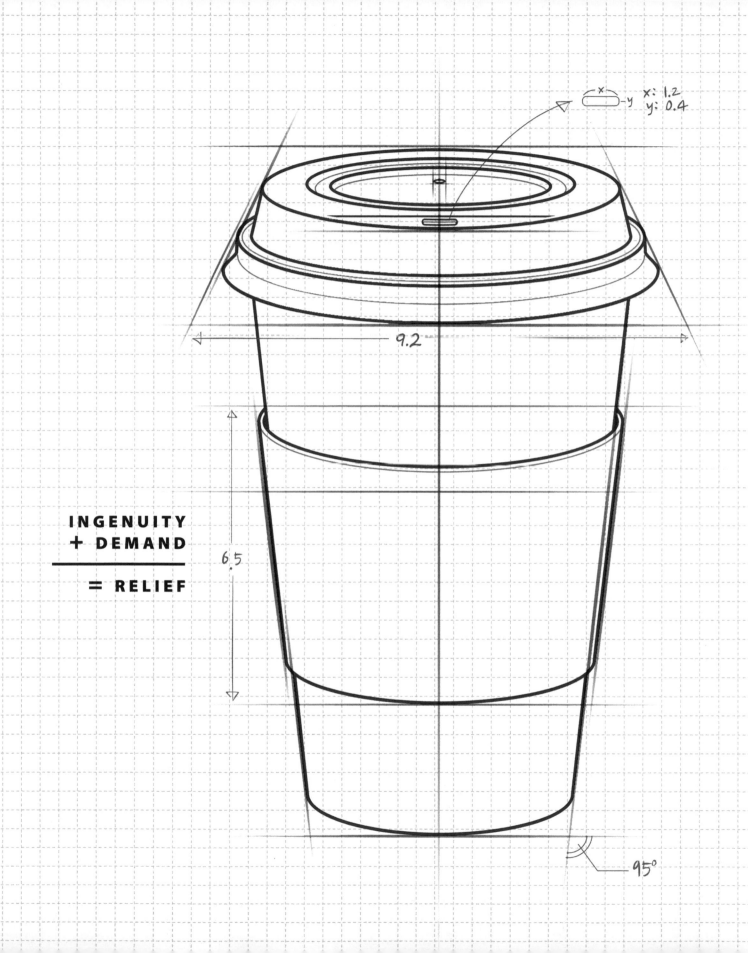

x: 1.2
y: 0.4

9.2

INGENUITY
+ DEMAND
———————
= RELIEF

6.5

95°

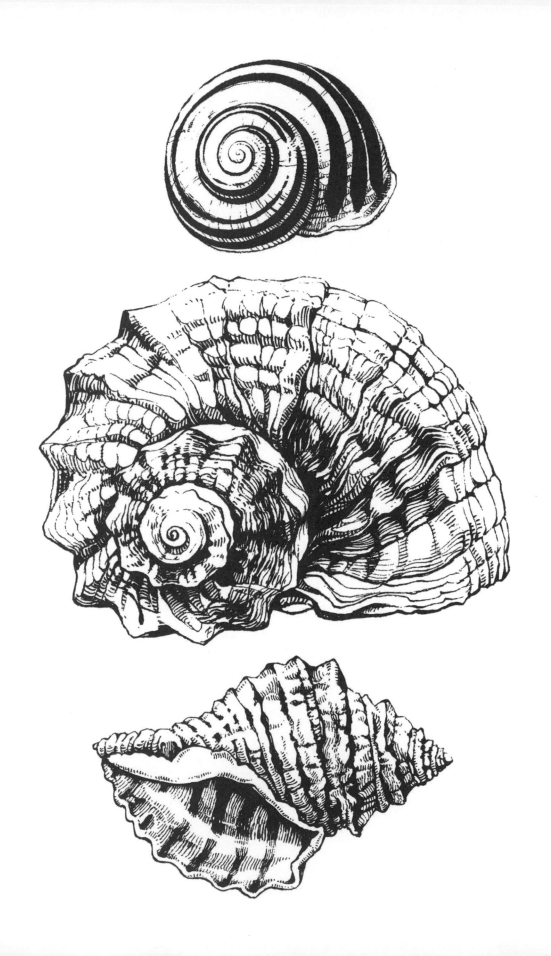

**LOOK THROUGH THOSE SHELLS
YOU PICKED OFF THE BEACH
TWENTY YEARS AGO**

DREAM
A LITTLE
MORE

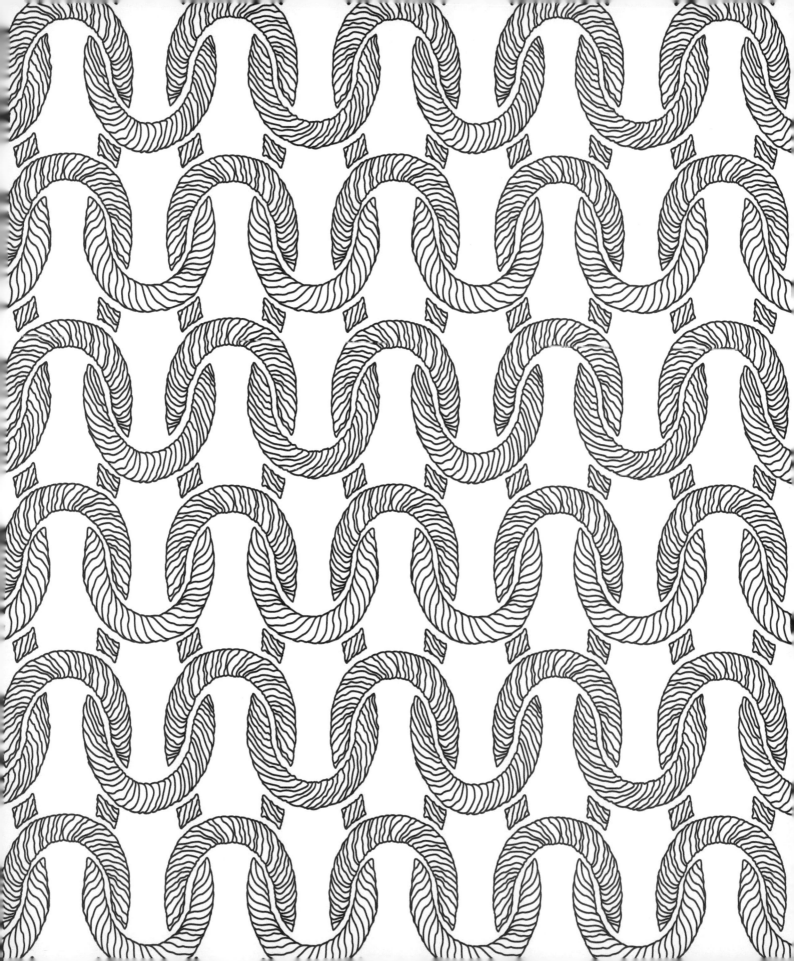

PERSPECTIVE IS IMPORTANT

MAYBE
YOU JUST HAVE A BUG
(OR A VIRUS)

**DON'T SWEAT IT.
NO ONE IS PERFECT.**

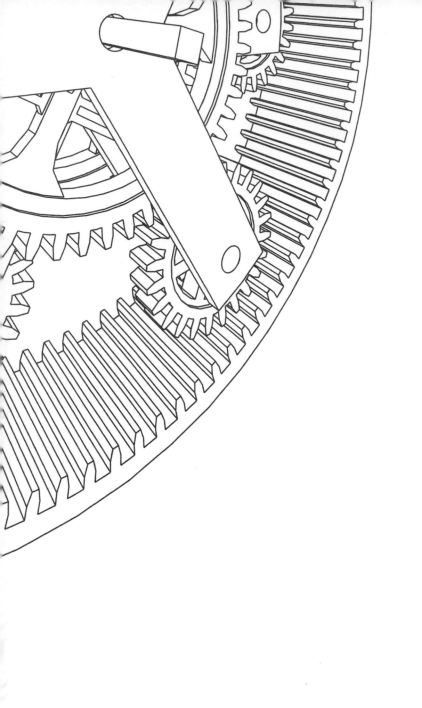

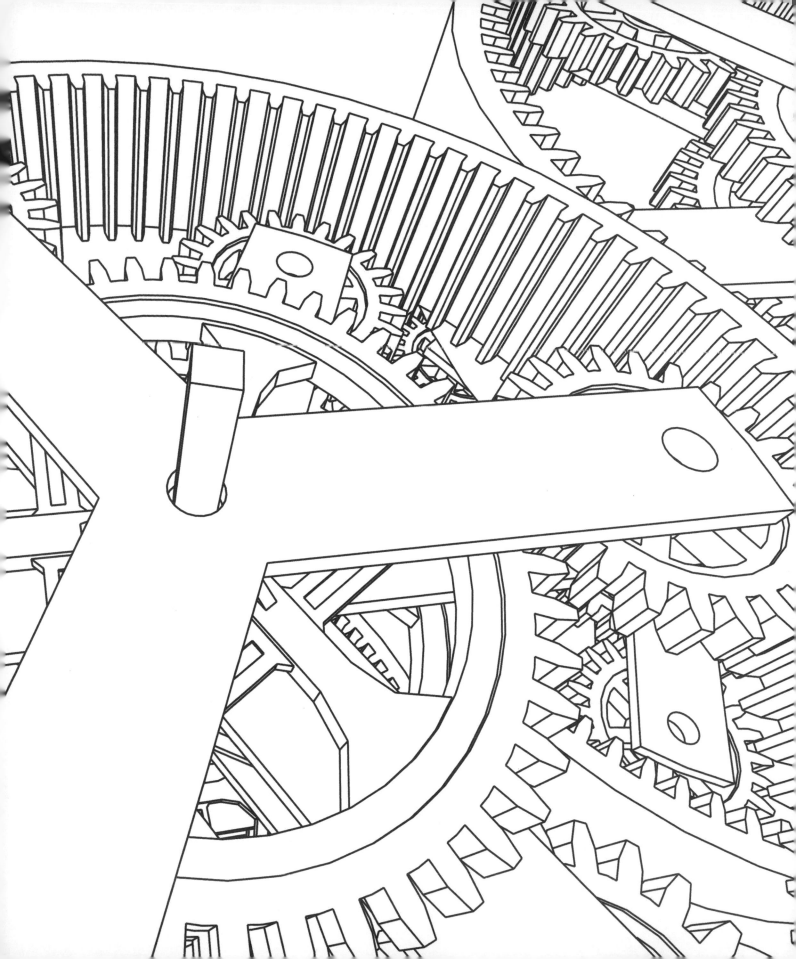

TRY GROWING A BEARD

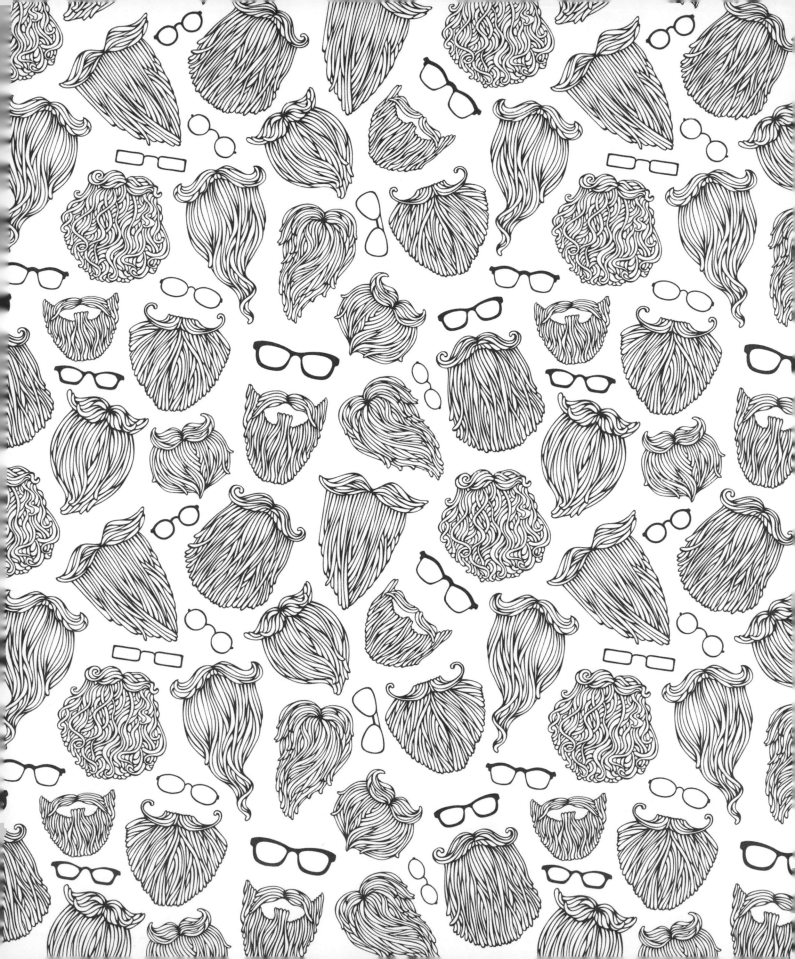

ENJOY SOME TIME AT HOME
(OR CASTLE)

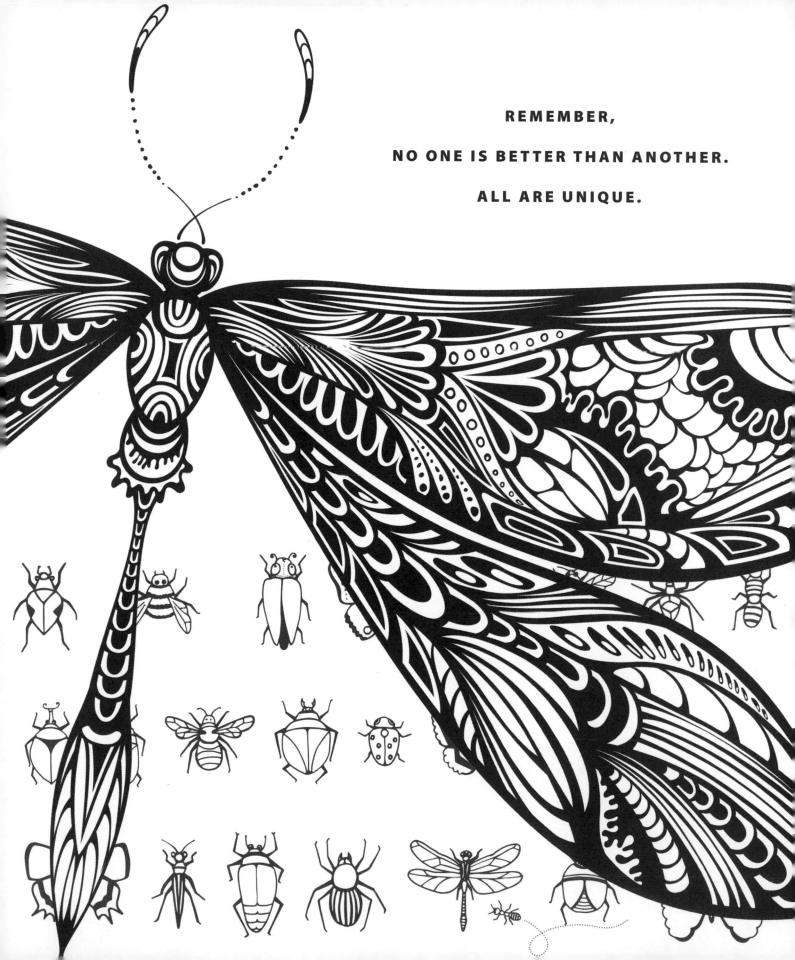

REMEMBER,

NO ONE IS BETTER THAN ANOTHER.

ALL ARE UNIQUE.

SOMETIMES YOU **DO** HAVE GREAT IDEAS.

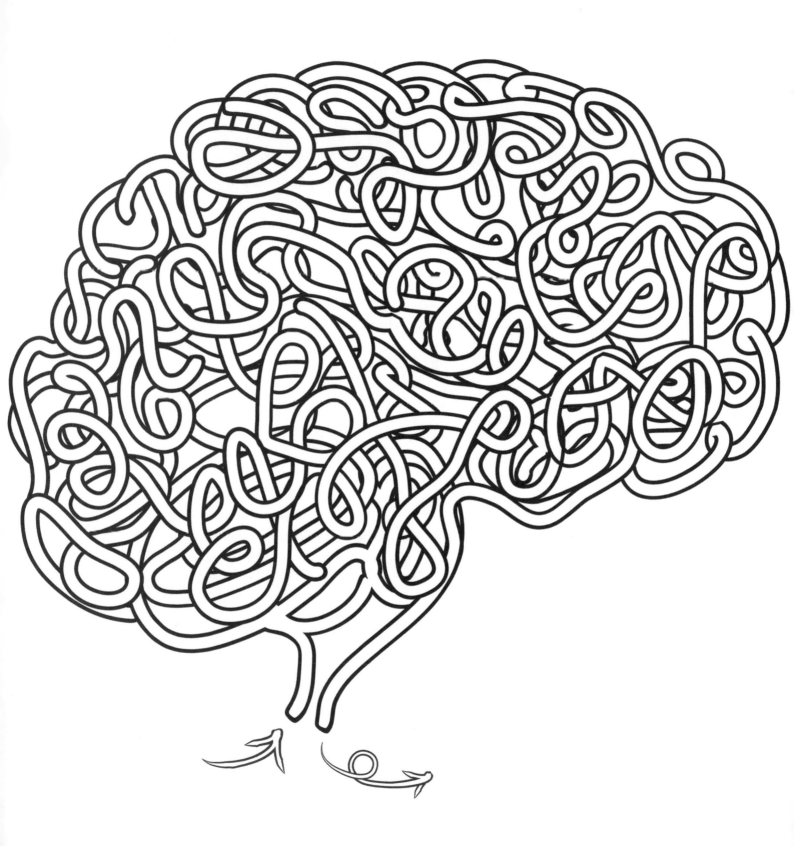

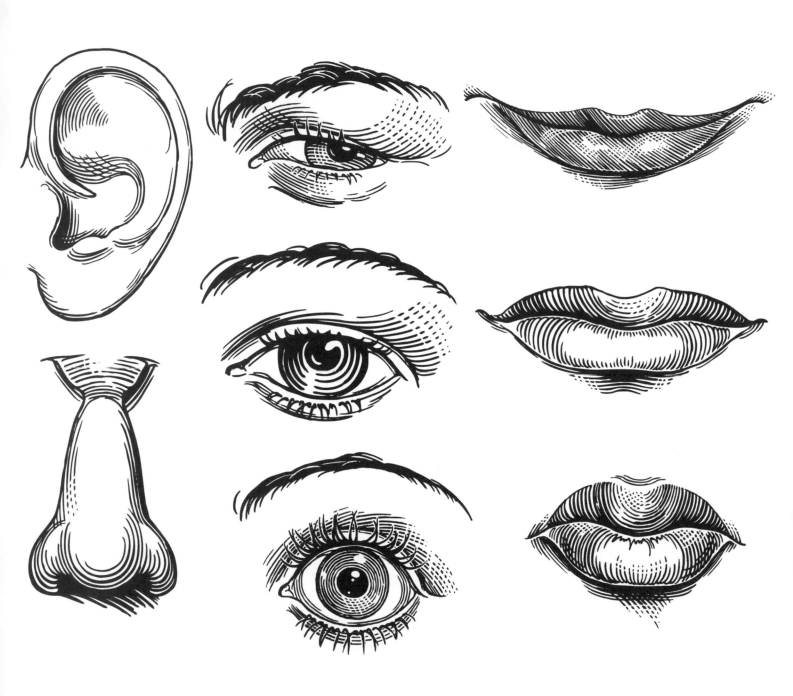

WHAT'S YOUR FACE TELLING OTHERS

BURN
SOME
ENERGY

TOMORROW COULD BE A BETTER DAY